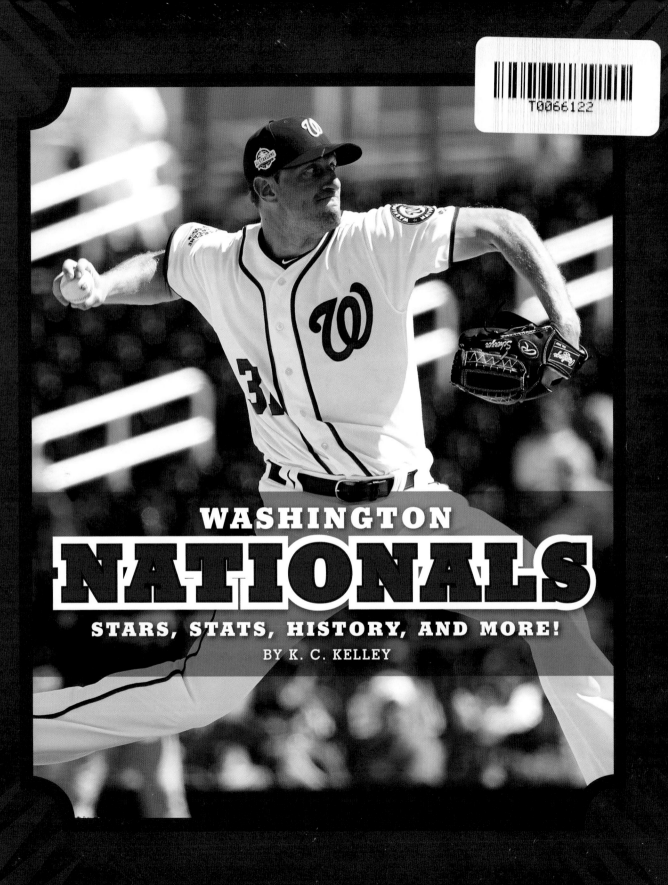

WASHINGTON
NATIONALS
STARS, STATS, HISTORY, AND MORE!

BY K. C. KELLEY

The Child's World®
childsworld.com

Published by The Child's World®
1980 Lookout Drive • Mankato, MN 56003-1705
800-599-READ • www.childsworld.com

ISBN 9781503828438
LCCN 2018944859

Printed in the United States of America
PAO2392

Photo Credits:
Cover: Joe Robbins (2).
Inside: AP Images: Mike Janes/Four Seam Images 20;
Newscom: David Seelig/Icon SMI 9, Kevin Dietsch/UPI 5,
17, Mark Goldman/Icon SW 19, Samuel Stringer/Icon SW
27; Joe Robbins 6, 10, 13, 14, 23, 24, 29.

About the Author

K.C. Kelley is a huge sports
fan who has written more
than 100 books for kids. His
favorite sport is baseball.
He has also written about
football, basketball, soccer,
and even auto racing! He lives
in Santa Barbara, California.

On the Cover

Main photo: Star pitcher
Max Scherzer;
Inset: Catcher Gary Carter of the
Montreal Expos, which became
the Nationals in 2005.

CONTENTS

GO, NATIONALS!

Some fans call baseball "America's game." So it makes sense that there is a team in the nation's **capital**. The Washington Nationals play in Washington, D.C. They continue a long baseball tradition there. A team called the Senators played there from 1901 to 1960. Today, the Nationals are trying to bring a championship to D.C. Let's meet the Nats!

The Nationals hosted the 2018 All-Star Game. ➤
Washington star Bryce Harper won the Home Run Derby!

WHO ARE THE NATIONALS?

The Nationals play in the National League (NL). That group is part of Major League Baseball (MLB). MLB also includes the American League (AL). There are 30 teams in MLB. The winner of the NL plays the winner of the AL in the **World Series**. The Nationals are still waiting for their first World Series title. Today's team is packed with talent, so that first title might come soon!

◄ *Ryan Zimmerman has been a big part of the Nationals since 2005.*

WHERE THEY CAME FROM

In 1969, the Montreal Expos became a new team in MLB. The Expos were the first MLB team to play in Canada. In 2005, the team moved to Washington, D.C. It was the first team in the capital since 1960. Fans were very excited to welcome back baseball. The team changed its name to the Nationals. Of course, it kept the red, white, and blue colors!

Vladimir Guerrero starred for the Expos ➤
when they played in Montreal.

WHO THEY PLAY

The Nationals play in the NL East Division. The other teams in the NL East are the Atlanta Braves, the Miami Marlins, the New York Mets, and the Philadelphia Phillies. The Nationals play more games against their division **rivals** than against other teams. In all, the Nationals play 162 games each season. They play 81 games at home and 81 on the road.

◄ *Speedy shortstop Trea Turner is sure to help the Nationals win.*

WHERE THEY PLAY

Nationals Park opened in 2008. Before then, the team played at RFK Stadium, home to an NFL team. For the team's first game, President George W. Bush threw out the **first pitch**. Nationals Park has room for more than 41,000 fans. The park is located near the Navy Yard. Because of that, the team blasts a loud submarine horn after a home run by the Nats!

Nationals Park is located just south of the U.S. Capitol building. ➤

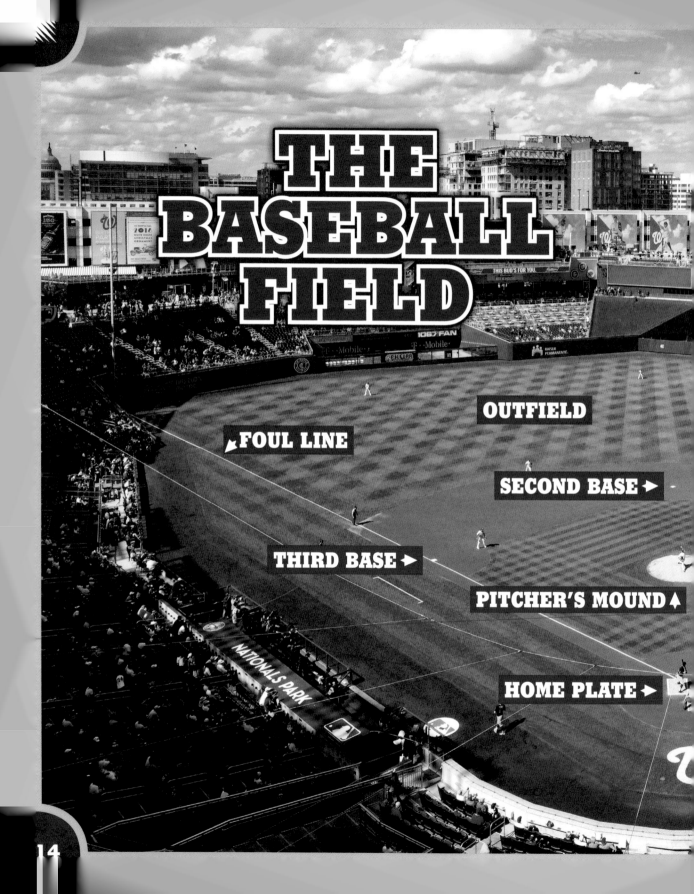

THE BASEBALL FIELD

OUTFIELD

◄ **FOUL LINE**

SECOND BASE ►

THIRD BASE ►

PITCHER'S MOUND ▲

HOME PLATE ►

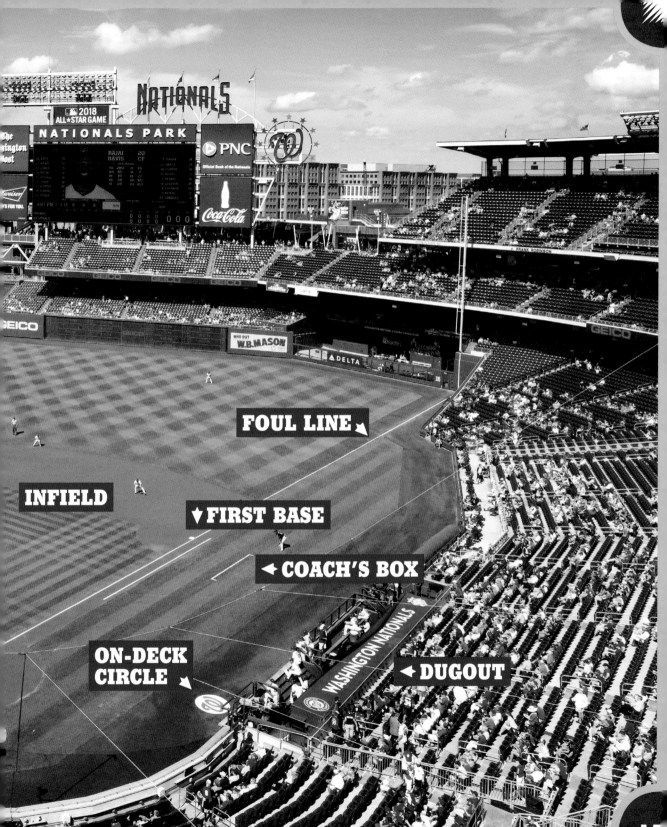

FOUL LINE

INFIELD

FIRST BASE

COACH'S BOX

ON-DECK CIRCLE

DUGOUT

BIG DAYS

he Nationals have not had a long history, but they have had some big days. Here are a few of them.

1991—This game was from the team's Expos days. Dennis Martinez pitched a **perfect game**. He did not allow a single baserunner. The Expos beat the Los Angeles Dodgers 2–0.

2012—The Nationals won their first NL East title with a team-record 98 wins. They lost in the playoffs, but it was a great season.

▲ *Zimmermann was hit with water by celebrating teammates.*

2014—Jordan Zimmermann threw a no-hitter! It was the final game of the season. Next stop, the playoffs, as the Nationals had the NL's best record.

TOUGH DAYS

ike every team, the Nationals have had some not-so-great days, too. Here are a few their fans might not want to recall.

1981—The Expos made it to the NL Championship Series. They were one win away from the World Series. Then Dodgers outfielder Rick Monday hit a homer that won the game for Los Angeles.

2009—In their second season in a new ballpark, the Nats disappointed their fans. The team lost 103 games. That is the most in their D.C. history.

▲ *Anthony Rendon was tagged out in a 2014 playoff loss to the Giants.*

2014—A great season ended badly. The team was tops in the NL. In the playoffs, though, they lost in the first round to the San Francisco Giants.

MEET THE FANS!

Nationals fans waited a long time for baseball to return. The fans come out in big numbers to cheer for their favorites. Several U.S. presidents have come to games. They live in Washington, D.C., too! All the fans get help from the team's **mascot**. Like the national bird, Screech is a bald eagle! A big hit at Nationals games is the presidents' race. People in giant foam heads sprint around the field.

◄ *Thomas Jefferson, Theodore Roosevelt, and Abraham Lincoln are among the racing presidents.*

HEROES THEN

This team has had two homes. So it has two sets of great players. In Montreal, catcher Gary Carter was one of the all-time greats. Andre "The Hawk" Dawson was an all-around great player. Outfielder Rusty Staub was known as "Le Grand Orange." That means The Big Redhead in French! First baseman Ryan Zimmerman is a star of yesterday and today. He was part of the Nationals from their first season in D.C.

Carter was a seven-time All-Star in 10 seasons in Montreal. ➤

HEROES NOW

Slugging outfielder Bryce Harper is one of baseball's best players. He was the 2012 **Rookie** of the Year and 2015 NL Most Valuable Player. Shortstop Trea Turner and outfielder Juan Soto are great young players. Pitcher Max Scherzer has won two **Cy Young Awards** with the Nats. He's a strikeout-throwing machine! Stephen Strasburg is another powerful pitcher.

◀ *Max Scherzer is probably the best pitcher in baseball right now.*

GEARING UP

**B**aseball players wear team uniforms. On defense, they wear leather gloves to catch the ball. As batters, they wear hard helmets. This protects them from pitches. Batters hit the ball with long wood bats. Each player chooses his own size of bat. Catchers have the toughest job. They wear a lot of protection.

THE BASEBALL

The outside of the Major League baseball is made from cow leather. Two leather pieces shaped like 8s are stitched together. There are 108 stitches of red thread. These stitches help players grip the ball. Inside, the ball has a small center of cork and rubber. Hundreds of feet of yarn are tightly wound around this center.

◄ CATCHER'S MASK AND HELMET

◄ CHEST PROTECTOR

◄ WRIST BANDS

◄ CATCHER'S MITT

◄ SHIN GUARDS

CATCHER'S GEAR

TEAM STATS

ere are some of the all-time career records for the Washington Nationals. All of these stats are through the 2018 regular season.

HOME RUNS	
Ryan Zimmerman	264
Vladimir Guerrero	234

RBI	
Ryan Zimmerman	988
Tim Wallach	905

BATTING AVERAGE	
Vladimir Guerrero	.323
Tim Raines	.301

STOLEN BASES	
Tim Raines	635
Marquis Grissom	266

WINS	
Steve Rogers	158
Dennis Martinez	100

SAVES	
Jeff Reardon	152
Chad Cordero	128

Strasburg has a shot at the top spot on the Nationals strikeout list. ➤

STRIKEOUTS

Steve Rogers	1,621
Stephen Strasburg	1,444

GLOSSARY

capital (KAP-ih-tull) the city that is home to a nation's or a state's government

Cy Young Awards (SY YUNG uh-WARDZ) honors given to the top pitcher in each league

first pitch (FURST PICH) a ceremony before a game starts in which a person throws a ball from the mound

mascot (MASS-kot) a costumed character that helps entertain fans

perfect game (PER-fekt GAYM) a game in which the starting pitcher does not allow a single baserunner to the other team

rivals (RYE-vuhlz) people or groups competing for the same thing

rookie (RUH-kee) a pro player in his or her first season

World Series (WURLD SEE-reez) the annual championship of Major League Baseball

FIND OUT MORE

IN THE LIBRARY

Connery-Boyd, Peg. *Washington Nationals: The Big Book of Activities*. Chicago, IL: Sourcebooks Jabberwocky, 2016.

Corso, Phil. *Bryce Harper (Young Sports Stars)*. New York, NY: PowerKids Press, 2018.

Sports Illustrated Kids (editors). *Big Book of Who: Baseball*. New York, NY: Sports Illustrated Kids, 2017.

ON THE WEB

Visit our website for links about the Washington Nationals: **childsworld.com/links**

Note to Parents, Teachers, and Librarians: We routinely verify our web links to make sure they are safe and active sites. So encourage your readers to check them out!

INDEX